THE MIRACLE DIET

THE MIRACLE DIET

POEMS BY
carol RUMENS

CARTOONS BY
viv QUILLIN

BLOODAXE BOOKS

Poems copyright © Carol Rumens 1998
Cartoons copyright © Viv Quillin 1998

ISBN: 1 85224 418 6

First published 1998 by
Bloodaxe Books Ltd,
P.O. Box 1SN,
Newcastle upon Tyne NE99 1SN.

Bloodaxe Books Ltd acknowledges
the financial assistance of Northern Arts.

LEGAL NOTICE
All rights reserved. No part of this book may be
reproduced, stored in a retrieval system, or
transmitted in any form, or by any means, electronic,
mechanical, photocopying, recording or otherwise,
without prior written permission from Bloodaxe Books Ltd.
Requests to publish work from this book
must be sent to Bloodaxe Books Ltd.
Carol Rumens and Viv Quillin have asserted their right under
Section 77 of the Copyright, Designs and Patents Act 1988
to be identified as the authors of this work.

Cover printing by J. Thomson Colour Printers Ltd, Glasgow.

Printed in Great Britain by
Cromwell Press Ltd, Broughton Gifford, Melksham, Wiltshire.

Contents

9   It's a Free Country
10 The Famine Diet
11 The Emperor's New Diet
12 Manufacturer's Explanation
13 Yorkshireman's Suggestion
14 Bad Ads
15 Tips for Quick Weight-Loss
16 A Gurgle in the Supermarket
17 Snarl from the Farmyard
19 Matt the Ombudscat
20 Genetics
22 Yesterday (or The One-to-Seven Waist-Hips Ratio)
24 Mutterings from a Changing Room *No.1*
25 Miraculous Symmetry
26 Fat Sod's Law
27 Perceptual Paradox
28 Talking to My Mirror
29 It
30 They're Cuddly, But…
31 Excuses, Excuses
32 A Very Difficult Riddle
33 One Day, My Diorella
34 Mutterings from a Changing Room *No.2*
35 The Unwanted Fat-Cell's First Love-Poem
36 Battle-Chant of the True Flab-Fighter
37 The Ballad of the Wise Dragon
38 So What's the Problem?
39 From an Old Movie
40 Anorexic's Prayer
41 Ms Narcissus
42 When Do They Stop Running?
43 Mabel and the Time Diet
44 Mutterings from a Changing Room *No.3*

45 Psychoanalysis
47 Legend
48 Intimidation
49 Stop Looking and Start Living

    FROM *The Curvy Lines Anthology*
51 The Health Farm Called 'Inches Free'
52 To Some I Have Talked With by the Fire
53 If –
54 Song of the Two Sad Queens
56 Repeat After Me
57 This is just to say
58 The Bite
60 Botties in Metroland
61 Please Can I Have
62 Nursery Stuff

It's a Free Country

Who put the water in the low-fat cheese?
Who put the con in Conley?
Who put the arthritis in the jogger's knees?
           We did, the punters.

Who paid double for half the taste?
Who bought the booze without the buzz?
Who said to the surgeon: take another little bit of my waist?
           We did, the punters.

The Famine Diet

Some people say I can't lose weight,
But that's a load of crap.
Anyone can starve to death
– Ask this Calcutta chap.

I eat so sparingly, they moan,
But, Jesus, if they did,
They'd spend the whole day lying down
– Ask this Rwandan kid.

The Emperor's New Diet

One day they'll produce a no-calorie food
   Called 'One Thousand Flavours of Air'.
In an elegant packet, gold leaf on matt black, it
   Won't retail just any-old-where

But they'll sell them at Harrods, and quality outlets,
   Those 'One Thousand Flavours of Air'
So if you've the dosh, and you're brainless but posh,
   You can buy the reply to your prayer.

Manufacturer's Explanation

Yes, *fewer calories* costs more
'Cos calories are tricky.
We can't just nip 'em out like fleas;
They're stubborn and they're sticky.
And so we charge you for the time
It takes to send 'em packin',
And for the tests, in case some pests
Have managed to sneak back in.

Yorkshireman's Suggestion

Eat less.
Pay less,
Weigh less
– Eh, lass?

Bad Ads

Wish you looked sexier?
Try fast-acting *Anorexia*.

Take your coffee creamier.
Eat cake. Get *Bulimia*.

Tips for Quick Weight-Loss

Pluck your eyebrows, shave your armpits,
Cut those hangnails off your toes.
If your teeth are false, remove them
Either blow or pick your nose.

A Gurgle in the Supermarket

Fill me, thrill me, whispers Gut,
Celebrate this age of glut.
Though I'm just a little blob,
I'll get bigger. That's my job.
I'm not made of bone, but plastic;
I'm a beautifully elastic
Larder for lean times ahead
– Though more beer-fests come instead!

Snarl from the Farmyard

Don't talk to me about Eating Disorders!
Let's hear more about Manufacturing Disorders
And Marketing, and Profiteering, Disorders.

Does a battery chicken have an eating disorder?
Does a force-fed pig?

So what about the human population
Herded to the supermarket trough,
Urged to consume, consume,
With savage disregard for natural appetite?

Don't talk to me about Eating Disorders!
Tell me instead about the brave attempts
To create an Eating Order

And praise those who read the small print on the cartons,
Who 'cut down' and 'exercise'
And occasionally fast, and constantly worry.

They're bloody well right to worry.

Matt the Ombudscat

I'm Matt the Ombudscat
   And I'm writing *The Bad Tin Guide*.
If *you* buy tins for your Whiskered Ones,
   First study what's inside,
   And the treacherous tricks they hide.

Some boast of a top-notch taste
   And, yes, puss pleads for more,
But it's only the added caffeine
   That makes her purr and paw
   The lid. Withdraw! Withdraw!

Some smell of best minced beef,
   They're cheap as well – what luck!
But for every gram of protein
   There's cereal by the truck.
   Soon puss will walk like a duck.

Watch out, pet-poisoners!
   You're in the catalogue
Compiled by Matt the Ombudscat,
   That tiger of a mog.
   (He's not some thicko dog!)

Genetics

Mum used to say sugar was good for you.
She was glad if she gained a pound or two
On her one-week jaunt to Whitley Bay:
It proved she'd had a real holiday.
'Fat and Happy' was her belief
(She called her lean sister 'Skin and Grief').
Mum was twelve stone and lived till eighty –
But so did seven-stone Auntie Katie.

Yesterday
(*or* The One-to-Seven Waist-Hips Ratio)

Yesterday
In a murky jungle far away,
Homo Sapiens was heard to say:
Cor, look at that one, she's OK!

(Why
She
Makes him glow, I don't know: it's nature's way.
Neat
Wee
Waists, big bums, thrilled our cave-chums yesterday.)

Her backside
Gives a bloke a lovely sense of 'wide'
Like a pitcher where a thief could hide,
And stow his favourite jewels inside.

(Why, etc.)

Suddenly
Underneath the spreading banyan tree,
He was twice the man he used to be.
She shut her eyes and thought: why me?

(Why, etc.)

We're the same.
Even in Victoria's stuffy reign,
In all cultures you can bear to name,
The hour-glass figure is fair game.

(Why, etc.)

Yesterday
In a mossy cavern far away
Man's desire delivered our today.
We're just the shape of yesterday.

Mutterings from a Changing Room *No.1*

These are Size Ten – though I'm really an Eight
In spate.

*I was Sixteen, but now I'm a wonderfully mean
Fourteen.*

Miraculous Symmetry

Why aren't dieters ever lopsided?
   I've never noticed they are!
Hips, boobs, buttocks, etc.
   Somehow remain on a par.

Why shouldn't the left side diminish
   While the right refuses to budge?
Why aren't dieters ever uneven,
   Like bags of home-made fudge?

Fat Sod's Law

Diet gurus advertise:
Shrink that beer-gut! Slim those thighs!

But the scientists argue warmly
Fat-cells vanish uniformly!

Both are wrong. You lose weight first
From the bits that aren't your worst.

Areas you'd thought all right
Dwindle almost overnight

While the bad bits seem to grow
– First to come and last to go.

Perceptual Paradox

When I'm thin I think I'm fat
Pinching bits of this and that,
Saying: Christ, my tum's a joke,
Must cut down on Diet Coke.

When I'm fat, I peep more shyly
Into mirrors, nice and smiley,
Tuck my tail up, tilt my chin,
Think: Good Heavens, I'm quite thin!

Talking to My Mirror

Am I fat or am I thin?
Scrawny neck and double chin –
Jutting vein and squidgy fold –
Thin or fat?
      No, babe. Just old.

It

1

Some get it sucked away
Some have it tucked away
You might have yours trucked away
But I'd prefer mine
                fondled away.

2

Is it still a *feminist issue*
Even when it's a man-sized tissue?

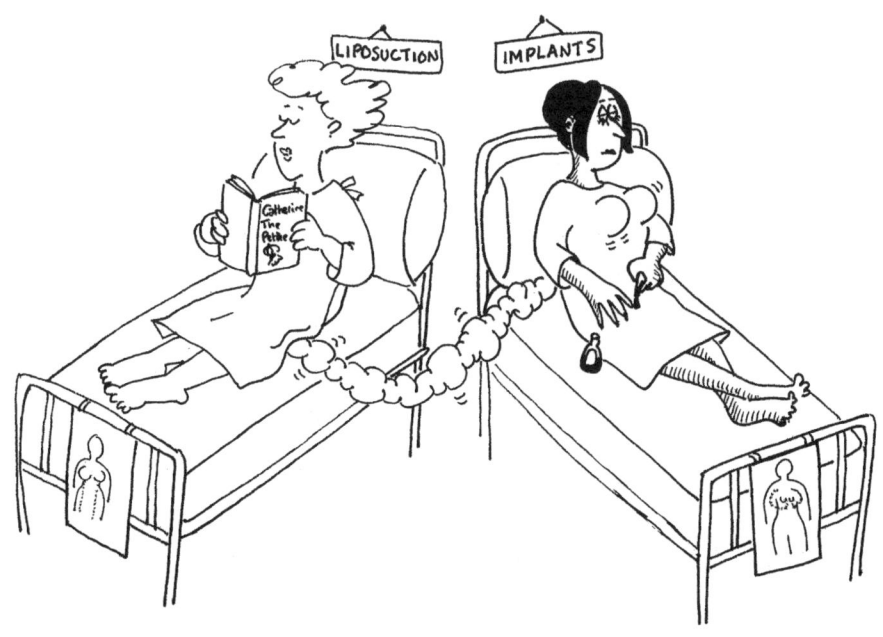

They're Cuddly, But…

Those men with their pregnant bellies
Wouldn't be bad at all,
If only the neighbouring willies
Weren't, comparatively, so small.

Excuses, Excuses

He's obese.
She's adipose.
They're steatopygous.
You're just gross.

Me? I've got these
BIG BONES.

A Very Difficult Riddle

Tried to leave home
   But had a gate problem.
Tried to get laid
   But had a date problem.
Tried to love myself
   But had a hate problem.

Guess what I've got now?

I've got a weight problem.

One Day, My Diorella

Some dream of a golden coach
And a princely love affair,
But I'm no Cinderella!
I'm dreaming that Diorella
One day will make some tights that reach
Above my pubic hair.

Mutterings from a Changing Room *No.2*

I had a wicked girdle
It pressed my stomach flat
But what it thrust towards my bust
– Let's not go into that.

Girdles are for nerdles.
What's wrong with your belly?
Some women have bay-windows.
Yours is just a telly.

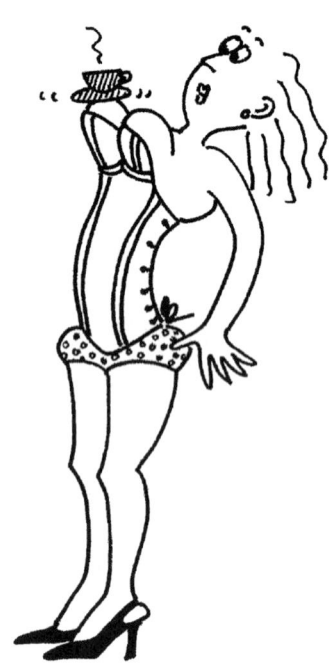

The Unwanted Fat-Cell's First Love-Poem

There's nothing worse than this
– To become a curse on the one you're closest to.
Does it need a poem?
Does it need a metaphor?
Ask any fat-cell with imagination
– They'll know at once how terrible it is
To become a curse on the one you're closest to.

Battle-Chant of the True Flab-Fighter

Some say there's good fat, called jolly poly unsat.
But fat's fat and that's that – and no fat is low-fat!

The Ballad of the Wise Dragon

I went out one morning on a bright summer's day,
My list said green salad, skimmed milk, Special K,
So I didn't look round at the Ming Take-Away,
Till the dragon who sits by the porch shouted: 'Hey!
   We've got plump crispy duck, just you try it.
   It won't make you fat though we fry it.
     No, it won't make you fat –
     You'll lose weight in fact
As long as it's part of your calorie-controlled diet.'

Well, I stopped where I stood; it was such a surprise
And I'd never accuse a live dragon of lies.
There was flame in his mouth, there was light in his eyes
As he said, 'Don't you fancy a bowl of fresh rice?
   There's oil in the wok to stir-fry it.
   Confucius, he say, *it no lie, it*
     Can all help you slim
     (How I goggled at him)
As long as it's part of your calorie-controlled diet.

So I bowed to the dragon and ordered the lot,
Spring rolls, duck and noodles, all glistening and hot,
And I counted the calories to the last jot.
When I'd counted one thousand, five hundred, I stopped
   And I shouted 'He's right! You can fry it,
   Munch chocolate, drink beer on the quiet.
     Consumption makes sense,
     And it needs no defence,
As long as it's part of a calorie-controlled diet.'

So What's the Problem?

I lose 5 lbs.
   I think: that's great!
But when I've reached
   My perfect weight,
I'm not so thrilled.
   I think: so what?
I'm only me,
   Size 10 or not.
I'm still fed up,
   Life's just the same,
Don't even have
   My bum to blame.

From an Old Movie

Falling for food again
   – Never wanted to
What's a girl to do?
   Can't help it.

Chocolates rush at me
   Like vultures to meat.
Soon, a big fat me
   Will gobble the petite.

Slurping ice-cream again
   – Häagen Dazs, of course,
Glugging down the sauce.
   Can't help it.

Anorexic's Prayer

Crusts of pain and sips of hate,
Save me from this sickening weight!
Make my mouth a bowl of dust.
Death can follow if it must.

Ms Narcissus

I was tender, I was slender,
I was lovely in his eyes,
But I'm lonely now, and haunted
– His new girlfriend's twice my size.
So I guess that I was lovely
In no other eyes but mine,
And it must be for my own lost,
Tender, slender self I pine.

When Do They Stop Running?

I hope one day before I die to see
A jogger who got out of breath, like me,
And had to stop and gasp against a tree:

A jogger sitting hunched up on a kerb,
His pulse irregular as a Martian verb,
His tee-shirt printed PLEASE DO NOT DISTURB.

When do they ever finish counting laps,
Those kneecap-flashers, those relentless chaps?
Please God, one day I'll see just one collapse.

Mabel and the Time Diet

There's nothing like a Meals-on-Wheels
   To stop you feeling lighter.
The funny thing, though – this old frock
   It don't get any tighter.

The helpers down the Centre joke:
   Mabel, you're in your prime.
I tell them: someone pinched me boobs.
   It was that bastard Time.

I used to be the chubby type,
   I couldn't get no thinner.
I cut out snacks, I cut out sweets,
   Then I cut out me dinner:

No good. But now the scales are stuck
   At seven measly stones
And what I see is what I'll be
   Before too long: me bones.

Mutterings from a Changing Room *No.3*

It's so itchy it's like rattan
– *dry-clean only* – and the pattern
Hurts my eyes. It's like a crossword,
    with some extra wiggly bits.
I'm not keen on lime and mustard
With a dash of pink, the rust'd
Suit me better but
      I'LL TAKE IT PLEASE IT'S WONDERFUL IT FITS!

Psychoanalysis

The fat man is sad
   He wanted to give birth
The fat woman is sad
   She wanted the earth
The fat child is sad
   It wanted to be the boss
And you – you're in denial
   If you don't give a toss.

Legend

There was once a woman
Who had a waist.
It's been displaced.

There was once a woman
Whose hip-bones shone.
Both are gone.

There was once a woman
Whose thighs
Must have been lies.

There was once a woman
Light as a glove.
She was in love.

There's a woman now
Who doesn't care.
So there.

Intimidation

In the sixties, the doctors warned:
You girls will get fat thighs
If you keep on wearing these little bits of skirts.
The body protects itself, you see.
Puts on extra fat against the cold.
Just wait till your thighs are wearing their winter woollies.
You'll be sorry you flaunted them at the elements.

In the sixties, I didn't care.
I showed off my Twiggy thighs
Till the fashions changed and hems kissed the pavements.
Since then, my thighs have gone on protecting themselves.
They're like Arctic explorers now.
They wear anoraks, windcheaters, mufflers, and carry ice-picks
And they terrify little bits of doctors.

Stop Looking and Start Living

Good old sixties generation
– Marched for women's liberation,
Burned their silly bras
But only 'cos they didn't need 'em:
Sisters, if you want real freedom,
Smash the looking-glass.

from The Curvy Lines Anthology

Poets have long been known for their skills at alcohol consumption. What is now beginning to emerge from our scholarly researches is that many of them have been equally gifted eaters. Perhaps this should not surprise us: the mouth, after all, is the sacred organ of the bard. This selection from the unpublished archives of such writers as William Psycho Williams and William Bunter Yeats will surely give a new dimension to twentieth-century literature. Whether refined gourmets like Elizabeth Binger-Bishop or demented scavengers of the fridge like Mr Williams, these poets reveal themselves to have been at the mercy of what Mr Williams evasively calls a 'food habit'. Some, of course, made strenuous if pathetic efforts to get in shape: see Mr Yeats's account of his gruelling stay at the Health Farm, 'Inches Free'. But at least one, John Bottyman, preferred to spectate as others jogged by. Compulsive eaters and compulsive dieters alike, all these poets will offer fascinated readers many delicious new insights into the human frailty of poetic genius...

The Health Farm Called 'Inches Free'

I will arise and go now, and go to 'Inches Free',
A single room will I book there, without mini-bar or Teasmade.
Nine enemas will I have there, and drink water endlessly,
And I'll run every hour to the pee-loud glade.

And I shall have some peace of mind, for peace of mind is won
When you drop below ninety calories a day,
When you feel your waistband loosen, and your belly shrinking
    down
(And you're payin' a quare sum to get that way).

I will arise and go now, for always I can hear
The slim young bard within me, sighing to be let out.
He's sighing as I order River Shannon Truite Meunière,
And when I'm drinking pints of Murphy's stout.

WILLIE BUNTER YEATS

To Some I Have Talked With by the Fire

While I worked out, gasping occasional rhymes,
My heart would brim with memories of the times
We'd sit in Dessie's snug, watching the fire
Burnish our glassware, call each other 'Liar!'
And sing 'The Girl Whose Underwear Was Green'
– Which was our version of 'Dark Rosaleen'.
Then one stout soul would glow with Fenian Flame,
Stride to the bar and yell the Ineffable Name:
'Dessie! Will ye stop polishin' that shelf!
We're after dyin' of thirst! Have one yerself!'

WILLIE BUNTER YEATS

If –

If you can keep your diet when those who love you
   Are pleading: but I bought your favourite cheese!
And say, as snooty waiters loom above you,
   'I'd simply like a small green salad, please.'
If you can hear, at times of celebration,
   That voice which, softer than a dropping pin,
Tells you to stop, and stand up to temptation,
   If you can join a Slimming Club – and slim:
If you can leave the bar while you're still thinking,
   And say I'm going for a run – and run,
And order fruit-juice while the lads are drinking
   Pints, you're just a bloody poofter, son.

'BASHER' KIPLING-CAKE

Song of the Two Sad Queens

Say there are ten thousand biscuits in the supermarket's
 aisles,
And if you lined up the bottles, they'd carry on for miles,
But there's no room in our trolley, my dear, no room for
 a single one.

We used to eat pizza and pancakes and choc-chip cookies
 galore.
Our calories burned like our young lust – but nothing burns
 any more:
We can't even look at the cakes, my dear, we daren't even
 look at the cakes.

We went from Gatwick to Tenerife on an off-peak package
 flight,
But the budget-size seats were too narrow, and the budget-
 size belts too tight,
And we didn't look good on the beach, my dear, we didn't
 look good at all.

We were standing outside a tapas bar, we didn't dare go in.
The salads were too well-dressed for us yet everyone there
 was thin.
They were the beautiful people, my dear, and they sneered
 at you and me.

We don't go out much any more and there's nothing on
 the telly
Except a man in a leotard, he's all biceps and taut belly.
He wants us to look like him, my dear, he wants us to look
 like him.

Dreamed we were going to heaven's ball, where the souls
 of the blest and brave
Were eating quiche and drinking juice and generally having
 a rave
But they didn't weigh more than eight stone, my dear,
 they didn't weigh more than eight stone.

Then down came a troop of angels, said 'Are you ready
 to die?'
And they opened the gates of heaven for us, but the gap
 was a needle's eye.
We were too full of sin to get in, my dear, we were much
 too full of sin.

AUDEN MAUDLIN

Repeat After Me

I will no longer believe what I'm told by the media.
The truth is, a lot of bones just makes you look weedier.
Who'd be a leaflet if they could be an encyclopaedia?

HOGDEN GNASH

This is just to say

I have eaten the plums
and the quiche
and the Mississippi
Mud-Pie, also

the oven-chips,
the paté,
yes, and the
custard

which was going off.
Forgive me.
I've got this
food habit.

WILLIAM PSYCHO WILLIAMS

The Bite
(for Alice Meths-Guzzle)

I cooked a tremendous fish,
and set him on my plate,
without chips, without any sauce at all.
I poked at his silvery skin,
mottled, like an old looking-glass,
and gazed at him.
He was innocent of carbohydrate,
yet I hesitated.
I was thinking: what about some butter?
What harm in a speck of butter?
Before I could stop myself,
I'd dabbed on a rather large pat
(it was larger than I'd intended)
and was watching the little gold tears
run this way and that.
I shivered. I couldn't move.
How many calories
had I just polluted him with?
His curled lip, his sullen
white eye seemed to mock me.
He was infested with calories!
I cut off his head.
And now my knife and fork
plunged easily into his flesh,
the protein-packed white flesh,
freckled with pepper, salt, dill
and a pinch of tarragon, shining
with melting lemony sunlight,
and a sense of deliciousness

flooded my palate, and my heart
was pounding, pounding, pounding,
and I took the first bite.

ELIZABETH BINGER-BISHOP

Botties in Metroland

Jogging bottoms joggling
In their jogging-bottoms,
Jogging-tops like lollipops
In matching fleecy cottons,

Lemon, sky and cyclamen,
Scarlet, mauve and lime,
Round the block they bravely bounce,
And round just one more time!

Jiggling tops and joggling bots
Jostling brave and bold.
Bulging eyes are boggling
– O joggly joys of jogging,
So jolly to behold!

JOHN BOTTYMAN

Please Can I Have

Please can I have a banana.
You thought I was going to say 'Man',
didn't you? But I don't want a man,
not even one who makes me fresh creamy curries
with lemon grass. I just want a
fat yellow banana.
No strings. No sperm. But rather a lot
of fat yellow calories.
OK?

SEMOLINA HILL

Nursery Stuff

don't like di sun
don't like di beach
don't want no lettuce
                (YUK)
don't want no peach

want to sit an' roast
by a big ole radiator
an' crunch buttered toast
like a bloomin' alligator

don't want to shop
don't want to show
                (UP)
don't want to party
don't want to know

want to snuggle down
wid a bottle of gin
and if yuh didn't bring no chips
                (YUM YUM)
yuh can't come in.

JEAN 'CHUNKA' CHEESE